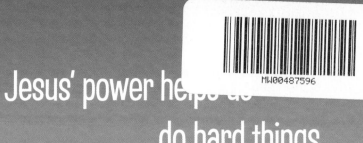

Jesus' power helps us do hard things.

"For I can do everything through Christ, who gives me strength." (Philippians 4:13)

👈 Meet Ramsey

TOUGH STUFF!

My name is Ananias, and Jesus asked me to do something really hard! Thankfully, I didn't have to do it by myself—Jesus was with me, giving me the power to do it!

Sometimes in life, you *have* to do hard things. And other times, you can choose whether or not you want to. Are there some hard things you'd try to do some day? Fill in the faces to show what you think about the tough stuff below.

You Want Me to Do *What?*

☹ 😐 🙂 ...ave

☹ 😐 🙂 ...arks

☹ 😐 🙂 S... ...e world's ...test roller coaster

☹ 😐 🙂 Climb a tall mountai...

☹ 😐 🙂 Drive a race car

☹ 😐 🙂 Run through fire

☹ 😐 🙂 Wrestle an alligator

☹ 😐 🙂 Run a marathon

☹ 😐 🙂 Ski an Olympic ski ju...

☹ 😐 🙂 Eat a grasshopper

☹ = I'll never do tha...

😐 = I might try tha...

🙂 = I can do that!

Read Ananias' story right here!

4

EYE OPENER

ACTS 9:1–19

BY ~ANANIAS~

SAUL.

His name made most Christians shake and shiver in their sandals! And I quaked and quivered right along with them. Even though I lived a long way from Jerusalem, I'd heard the scary stories. Saul hated Jesus' followers. He hunted down believers and sent them to jail. And if he didn't throw them in jail, he'd help toss them in the grave.

Saul was one scary dude.

And Jesus wanted *me* to go pay Saul a visit?

"But Lord!" I prayed, "I've heard so many stories about the terrible things he's done to believers like me. He arrests every Jesus-follower he finds!"

Jesus' voice was clear, "I have special plans for Saul. He's going to bring the good news to people everywhere."

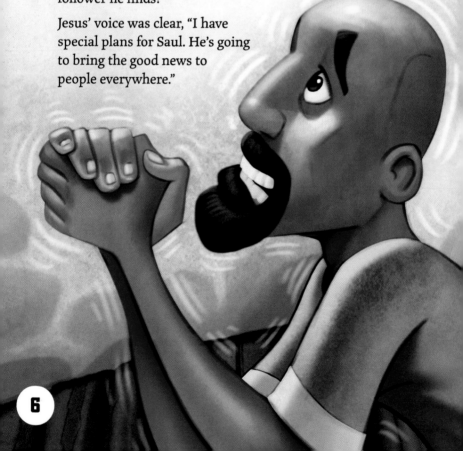

I learned the scoop on what had happened to Saul. He'd been on the road from Jerusalem, coming to arrest more believers in Damascus. But Jesus appeared to him in a bright light, and Saul went blind. Saul's friends had to lead him the rest of the way to Damascus, where he waited in darkness for three days.

And now Jesus wanted me to go pray for Saul?

Gulp.

AS frightened as I was, I knew I needed to trust Jesus no matter what. If Jesus asked me to give Saul his sight back, then I needed to do it—even if that meant Saul putting me in jail.

I went to the house of a man named Judas, who lived on Straight Street. When I saw Saul, he looked nothing like the raging bully I'd imagined. He looked tired and hungry— after all, he hadn't had anything to eat or drink for three days!

I gently put my hands on his head.

"Saul, my friend, Jesus sent me so you can see again and so you can be filled with God's Holy Spirit," I said.

Just like that, something strange— like scales—fell off Saul's eyes. He blinked in the bright light.

"I can see!" he said!

I could tell right away that he could see— not just with his eyes but also with his heart.

Saul wanted to be baptized...and to have a snack. (Three days is a long time to have an empty belly!) Soon Saul became one of Jesus' most faithful followers, helping people everywhere see the light of Jesus in a whole new way.

Sometimes Jesus wants us to do things that are hard. Like becoming friends with someone you don't like very much. Or forgiving someone who hurt you. Or stopping a bad habit.

But if Jesus wants us to do something, he always gives us the power to do it. Jesus will be with us all the way, just like he was with me went I went to visit Saul for the first time. I was scared and unsure, but I had Jesus' power with me the whole time.

Doing the right thing can seem hard sometimes. Maybe it's challenging to be patient with a younger brother or sister. Maybe it's hard for you to control yourself when it comes to watching screens too much or eating unhealthy food. But you know what? Jesus' power can give you the power to do those hard things!

If you trust Jesus and ask him to help you, Jesus always will.

⚙ ANANIAS ⚙

Jesus' power gives us hope.

"So be strong and courageous, all you who put your hope in the Lord!" (Psalm 31:24)

👉 Meet Ava

MAP YOUR WORLD

I'm Paul, and God sent me on *incredible* journeys around the world to tell about his love, power, and hope. Your world needs the hope of Jesus, too.

Circle some of the places you live. Think about your neighborhood, your family's farm, your city block—wherever you live, play, and spend time. As you do, think of the people around you who need Jesus' power to give *them* hope!

12

Check out Paul's adventures on the next page!

A PERFECT STORM

ACTS 27

BY PAUL

THE sails snapped in the wind, and the ship shook in the wild waves. Storm clouds swelled in the dark sky. I'd sailed the seas plenty of times as a missionary who brought the good news of Jesus to people far away. But now I was going on a very different kind of trip. This time I traveled as a prisoner, heading to Rome. There I'd stand trial for teaching people about Jesus. And right now the weather seemed as frightening as my future!

The weather caused trouble almost from the beginning. Over and over, the wind blew us off course. I had a strong feeling that we needed to stop for a while, so I talked to the crew.

"If we keep going like this, we're only going to run into trouble. We'll lose our cargo, the ship will wreck, and our lives will be in grave danger," I warned them.

But most captains don't take sailing advice from prisoners.

So we kept going.

Sure enough, the weather got downright dangerous. Fierce storms blew in from every direction and battered our boat. It got so bad that the sailors had to toss most of our supplies overboard. After hard days and sleepless nights, everyone felt tired, hungry, and most of all...afraid.

They were losing hope, and fast.

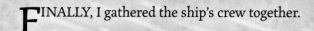

FINALLY, I gathered the ship's crew together.

"You should have listened to me. I told you things would get bad," I said to them. "But don't lose hope! God's angel told me last night that I will make it to Rome for my trial, and everyone with me on this ship will be safe, too. And I always believe God! Even though our ship will crash on an island, God will save all our lives."

The winds kept howling, and the sea kept tossing us back and forth. The sailors worked hard to keep the ship afloat, but their muscles burned and their bellies growled. Worry and fear shadowed their eyes. So I spoke up again.

"We've been fighting this horrible weather for two weeks!" I said. "You've been so scared that you haven't eaten this whole time. Let's eat something and forget about our troubles. Trust me! You're all going to be okay!"

Then I took some bread, thanked God for it, and ate a piece. Pretty soon, everyone on board was eating and feeling much better.

Sure enough, our ship wrecked on an island. But every single crew member and prisoner made it safely to shore. God *had* saved us all!

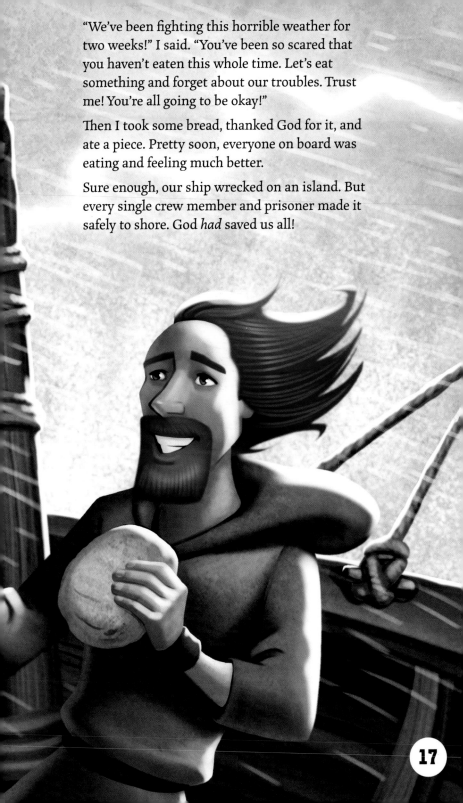

I've been through some very scary situations in my life. Angry crowds beat me. Soldiers locked me up. A poisonous snake even bit me! But every time, God was with me. I never lost hope because I knew that I carried Jesus' power everywhere I went.

Jesus' power gives me hope, and it should give you hope, too. Hope means believing that something good is going to happen. And there's nothing better to put your hope in than God.

You're going to go through some tough times in your life. Maybe you already have. When you put your hope in God, you can be sure that something good is waiting for you on the other side.

PAUL

Jesus' power helps us be bold.

"He gives power to the weak and strength to the powerless." (Isaiah 40:29)

Meet Sierra

GO FOR THE BOLD

I'm Peter! My friend John and I got to boldly share about Jesus—even though it meant we ended up in prison. I *love* talking about Jesus!

Maybe you're not sure about boldly telling people what you believe. Or maybe there are other things you're unsure about doing. Color in the lights to show how bold *you* feel about doing the things below! Red means "no way," yellow means "hmmm, maybe" and green means "go for it!"

Color in the lights to show what you think about the stuff below.

Do you want to...
- sing in a rock band?
- write a book?
- drive a bulldozer?
- train a dog?
- play quarterback?
- fly an airplane?
- perform surgery?
- preach a sermon in church?

Would you wear this costume?
- princess
- ninja
- cowboy or cowgirl
- clown
- villain
- soldier
- robot

Peter and John's true story starts here!

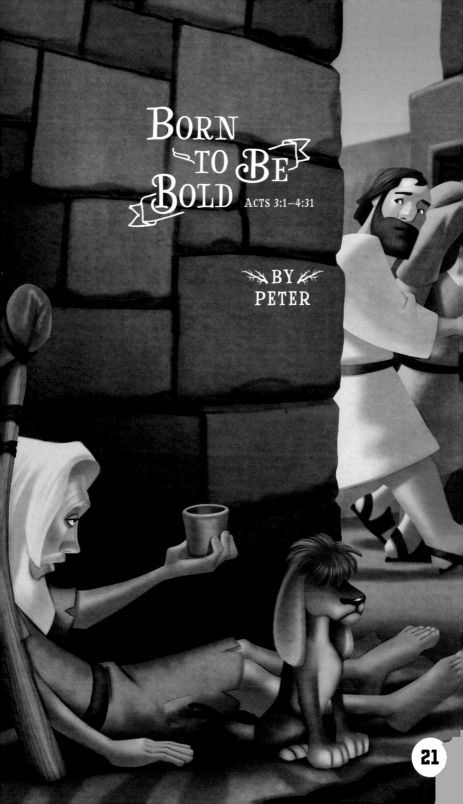

BORN TO BE BOLD

ACTS 3:1–4:31

BY PETER

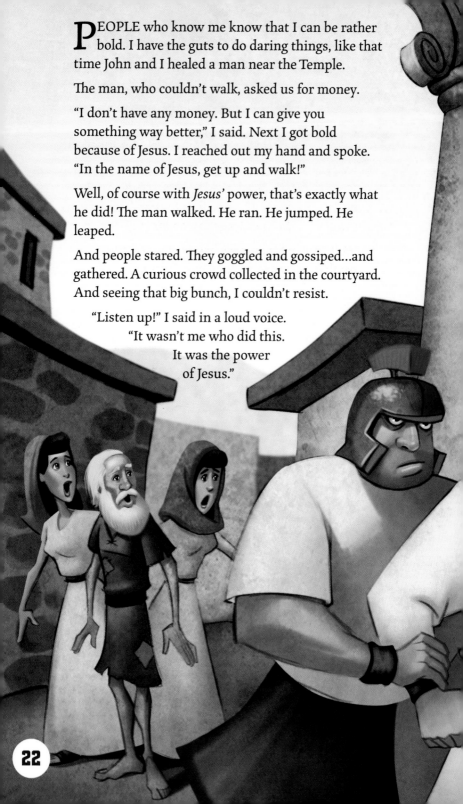

PEOPLE who know me know that I can be rather bold. I have the guts to do daring things, like that time John and I healed a man near the Temple.

The man, who couldn't walk, asked us for money.

"I don't have any money. But I can give you something way better," I said. Next I got bold because of Jesus. I reached out my hand and spoke. "In the name of Jesus, get up and walk!"

Well, of course with *Jesus'* power, that's exactly what he did! The man walked. He ran. He jumped. He leaped.

And people stared. They goggled and gossiped...and gathered. A curious crowd collected in the courtyard. And seeing that big bunch, I couldn't resist.

"Listen up!" I said in a loud voice. "It wasn't me who did this. It was the power of Jesus."

Then I told them the hard truth, whether they liked it or not. I scolded them for rejecting Jesus—for killing him on a cross instead of loving and following him.

"You didn't really know what you were doing. Besides, Jesus had to die so all the prophets' predictions would come true. But now's your chance to do the right thing! Say you're sorry for the wrong things you've done, and follow Jesus.

"Through faith in the name of Jesus, this man was healed. He walked for the first time in his life. Just think what faith in Jesus can do for you!"

Well...my boldness *may* have caused a little trouble. Pretty soon, John and I were surrounded by a different crowd. Of guards!

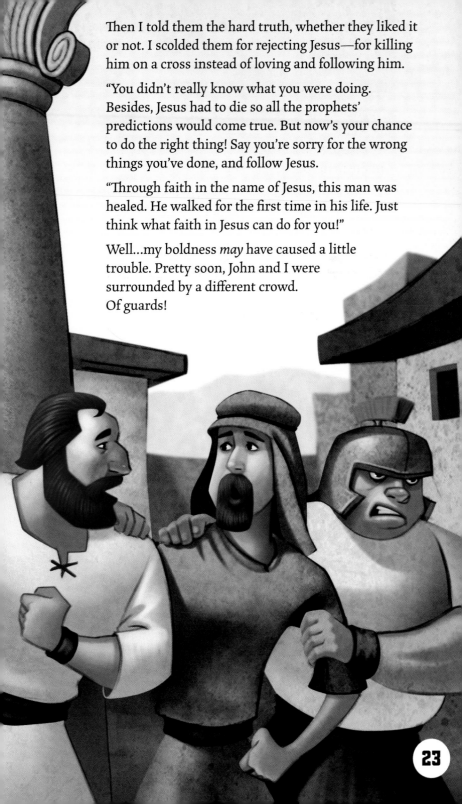

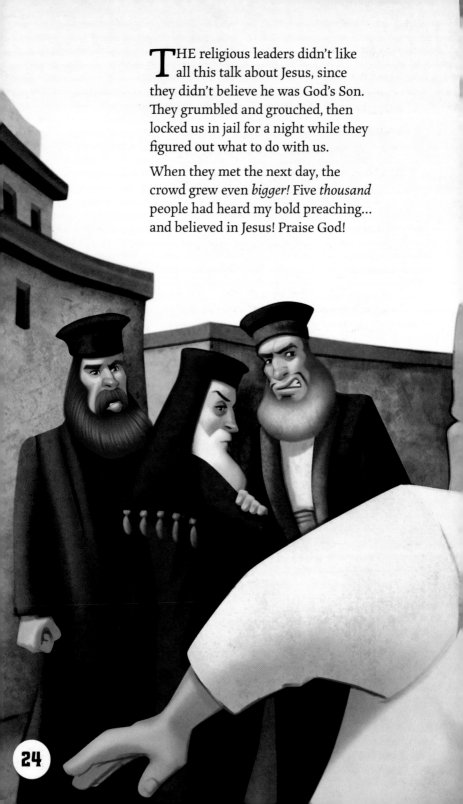

THE religious leaders didn't like all this talk about Jesus, since they didn't believe he was God's Son. They grumbled and grouched, then locked us in jail for a night while they figured out what to do with us.

When they met the next day, the crowd grew even *bigger!* Five *thousand* people had heard my bold preaching... and believed in Jesus! Praise God!

Of course, the religious leaders didn't think it was so great. Who were we— regular guys without any training or special schooling? How could *we* teach with such boldness and faith?

They mumbled and murmured in their meeting, scratching their chins and frowning as they pondered what to do. Finally, they shook their fingers at us, warning us not to speak in the name of Jesus. As if we could *ever* agree to *that!*

When we got home, we told other Christians what had happened. Then we prayed together, asking for even more boldness to tell the world about Jesus.

Just try to stop us!

I've lost track of the number of sick or hurt people I've met over the years. Some of them hurt on the outside, but plenty of them had broken and hurting hearts.

Jesus' power heals both of those, you know.

And sometimes all it takes is one person to stand out and make a difference; all it takes is someone to boldly speak up, giving the good news that Jesus' love and power are bigger than our hurts.

You may be shy about sharing. It might feel awkward or strange to tell someone, "Jesus loves you and can help." Maybe you even think people will laugh or make fun of you. Or perhaps you worry that you'll get in trouble! Remember that you don't face those fears alone. Jesus gives you *his* power…and *his* words! Whisper a prayer before courageously speaking up. He's right there with you!

Be bold, friends!

PETER

Jesus' power lets us live forever.

"The Spirit of God, who raised Jesus from the dead, lives in you." (Romans 8:11)

 Meet Finn

FRIENDS WITH GOD

God isn't just someone you study or learn about.
God wants *you* to be his real friend! A lot of people
make and wear friendship bracelets to show everyone
how much they love a friend. What do you think a
friendship bracelet with God would look like?
Draw it on the wrist here.

Check out Jesus'
story to see just
how much God
loves you!

EVERLASTING LIFE

MATTHEW
26:17—28:10

BY
JESUS

I'm going to tell you the most important story ever told. It won't be easy for you to hear. But I promise you this: It has the happiest ending in all the history of happy endings.

My name is Jesus. I'm God's Son, sent to earth to show God's unimaginable love for people. People had *heard* about God... I got to *show* them God! When I lived on earth, I taught, healed, made friends, loved, and did miracles that showed God's power. Not everyone believed me. Some called me a liar. Some plotted my death.

One of my dearest friends betrayed me.

Roman soldiers arrested me.

My friends abandoned me.

Alone, I stood trial in front of Pontius Pilate, the local governor. The people accused me of being a traitor, even though Pilate couldn't find anything wrong with me. But the angry mob shouted for my death. Just a week earlier they'd cheered for me as a king! Now they jeered for me as a criminal.

Guards beat me without mercy. They hit me and spit on me. They kicked me and whipped me over and over. They mocked me, calling me "King of the Jews," and draped a red robe over my shoulders. Then they made a crown out of sharp thorns and rammed it on my head.

I could've stopped them.

I had the power to put an end to it.

But I knew this was God's plan.

THE guards made a big cross out of wooden beams. Even though I had no strength left, they forced me to carry that cross. Its rough wood scraped my skin. My weakened body struggled against the weight. When I finally couldn't go any farther, they made another man carry it for me.

I stumbled up a hill to the Place of the Skull. I knew what came next. I knew it would be nearly unbearable. The soldiers gave me a bitter drink to ease the pain, but I wouldn't take it. I needed to endure every jolt, every stab, every sting.

When they laid me on my back on the cross, my whole body winced in agony. But nothing hurt more than the nails. The soldiers nailed my hands and feet, one at a time, to the rough wood.

"If you're the Son of God, why don't you save yourself?" they shouted.

But they didn't know. They didn't understand that this was God's plan. Worst of all, they didn't realize how much I loved them. Every tear and every drop of blood was for *them*.

THE sky turned black as I struggled to breathe. This frail, human, broken body didn't have much life left. The end was close.

I hung my head, unable to take another breath.

The moment I died, things got scary. The ground shook. Rocks split apart. People wept. The curtain in the Temple sanctuary split in half. Tombs opened up, and dead people began to come back to life.

The soldiers got scared.

One whispered, "This man truly was the Son of God!"

Later, a kind man named Joseph took my limp body off the cross. He gently wrapped it in cloths, treating me with love and respect. Then he laid me in his own tomb— sort of like a cave carved out of the rocks.

Even though I was dead, my enemies *still* worried! They'd heard people talk about me rising from the dead. They thought my followers might come to steal my body and claim I wasn't dead anymore. So they rolled a giant stone in front of the tomb entrance and placed two guards there to make sure nothing happened.

But something did happen.

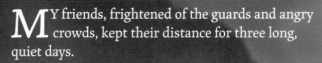

MY friends, frightened of the guards and angry crowds, kept their distance for three long, quiet days.

As soon as the sun cracked the morning sky on the third day, an earthquake rattled the tomb as one of God's radiant angels swept down and rolled the stone away. Then he hopped up and sat on it!

Shocked, the guards shook like crazy...and then fainted!

Just then Mary Magdalene and my other friend named Mary came to visit the tomb. Their teary eyes grew wide when they saw the dazzling angel standing there! Their jaws dropped.

"Don't worry," said the angel. "Jesus isn't here anymore. He's alive again! Hurry and go tell his followers!"

Mary and Mary took one glance at the empty tomb… and then started running. Excitement, fear, surprise, wonder, and a thousand questions raced through their minds as their feet raced through the quiet streets. I just couldn't stay away!

"Greetings," I said.

Astonished—and a little scared—they rushed to me and wrapped me in huge hugs. After a moment, I looked them in the eyes.

"Don't be afraid! Go tell my brothers to leave for Galilee, and they will see me there."

I was alive.

Forever.

God loved the world so much that he gave *me…* for you.

I willingly went through the pain of the cross, the hurt of a criminal's death, because it was the only way to take away the barrier of sin between people and God. That's how much you mean to me, friend.

When you're my friend, we're friends forever. I've gone to make a home for my friends…and it's *amazing!* We'll be together forever. Even though your human body might not last forever, there's the hope of life *forever* with me in a beautiful place called heaven. I can't wait for you to see it!

JESUS

Jesus' power helps us be good friends.

"Love each other in the same way I have loved you." (John 15:12)

Meet Lawrence Elk

CREW VIEW

The first Christians really had to be good friends who got along and helped each other. Hey, you've made some new friends right here at Rocky Railway!

Use the faces below to draw *your* new group of friends. What makes each person special? fun? unique? As you draw, thank your new friends for helping *you* discover what it means to trust Jesus!

See how Jesus' first followers were good friends who helped each other!

Tech Tattoos ™

Laptop · Cell Phone · MP3 · Tablet · GPS

Ultra Removable Tattoos.
Customize your technology!

Laptop, Notebook & Tablet

ROCKY RAILWAY
JESUS' POWER PULLS US THROUGH

Cell Phone, Music Player,
Game Console, GPS & E-Reader

I PUT THE ★ FUN ★ IN
VBS FUN SHOP

TRUST JESUS

Group
VBS GROUPIE

I ♥ VBS

Something To Believe In

ACTS 2:42–47;
4:32–35

BY AN EARLY CHRISTIAN

THERE'S family...and then there are friends that are *like* a family.

That's us!

We call ourselves "believers" because we believe that Jesus is the way to having a close friendship with God. We're regular folks like anyone else, but we know that God loves us and sent Jesus to save us from all the bad things we've done.

But that's not all.

After Jesus came back to life and went up into heaven, God gave us a helper called the Holy Spirit so *we* would have the power to do all sorts of amazing things!

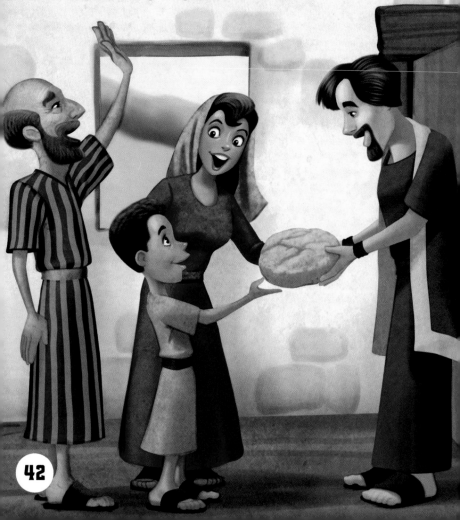

People can't stop talking about the things our leaders do in Jesus' name! These miracles are... well, miraculous!

But sometimes getting along with new friends can be hard. Jesus' power even helps us show love to each other, just like true friends do.

We worship God and pray together every day. We gather in friends' homes to eat. We sell our things and give the money to people who really need it. And we share everything we have. Caring for our family of believers brings so much joy!

IT'S not always easy to be a Christian. A lot of people don't believe like we do... and some of our friends have been put in prison. We *definitely* need each other.

We're united! We're like a body—even though a body has lots of different parts, they all work together to stay healthy and get things done. Everyone in our body lives at peace with each other because Jesus gives us the power to do it.

We work together to do the things we care about most—helping and loving other people. And none of us are "needy" because there's always another believer who's willing to sell their land and give the money to those who need it.

We're always on the lookout to add more and more friends to our body of believers. You can always tell who the believers are, because we're the ones who love each other, just like Jesus does.

Hallelujah!

When believers are doing what God tells them to do—worshipping together, sharing together, caring together, and giving together—there's nothing better in the world. We use Jesus' power to be good friends who truly love each other.

The best part is *anyone* can be a believer—including *you*. And when you believe, God gives you the Holy Spirit, too. That means you're filled with God's power to do amazing things, just like the very first believers.

I love being a believer! It's awesome! And I hope *you* will be a believer just like me.

AN EARLY CHRISTIAN

Buddy Tracks

Turn the page to see how to play this game that's mountains of fun for everybuddy!

How to Play Buddy Tracks

 Roll a pair of dice. Put your Buddy on the spot with the matching number. Follow the instructions on the spot. Make tracks to all the spots you can!

2—Choo Choo Chew You have 10 seconds to name as many foods as you can that start with the first letter of your name. Then point to someone to go next.

3—Laugh Track Have everyone put on their most serious face. Now see if you can get anyone to crack a smile. The first person who does takes the next turn.

4—Rocky Mountain Five Come up with a unique way to give a high-five, such as down *way* low, front of hand to back of hand, a "finger five," or "foot fives." The last person you high-five will go next.

5—Loco Motion! Everyone get up and change places. The last one to sit down takes the next turn.

6—Train Whistle Whistle a popular tune, TV theme song, or movie soundtrack. The first person to identify what you're whistling goes next. (If you can't whistle, it's okay to hum.)

7—Hawk Eye Spy Describe something in the room and see if anyone can correctly guess it with just 5 clues. The first person to correctly guess can decide who takes the next turn.

8—Story Connectors Start a story that begins with "Once upon a time..." The person to your right will add a sentence to the story, ending with "...and then..." Continue around the circle until the last person ends with "And they all lived happily ever after!" That person can take the next turn.

9—Whoo Whoo! Sing "She'll Be Coming Round the Mountain." The person to your left will come up with a different sound effect for "whoo whoo" and perform it during the song. That person can take the next turn.

10—Rocky Top Lawrence Elk has antlers, and Ramsey has horns. Tell what should grow out of *your* head! (Forks? A lightning rod? Faucets that produce soda pop?) The person across from you will go next.

11—All Aboard! Everyone puts a hand in the middle. Shout out a "team cheer" as your friends raise their hands. Someone wearing the same color as you will take the next turn.

12—Full Scream Ahead Come up with an ending to the cheer "Two, four, six, eight..." and cheer it as loud as you can. The last person who rolled an uneven number can go next.

Printed in the USA.
EAN 978-1-4707-6095-3

9 781470 760953

VBS PROGRAMMING